Events That Shaped America

Arriving at
Ellis Island

MaryLee Knowlton and Dale Anderson

Gareth Stevens Publishing
A WORLD ALMANAC EDUCATION GROUP COMPANY

Please visit our web site at: www.garethstevens.com
For a free color catalog describing Gareth Stevens Publishing's list of high-quality
books and multimedia programs, call 1-800-542-2595 (USA) or 1-800-387-3178
(Canada). Gareth Stevens Publishing's fax: (414) 332-3567.

Library of Congress Cataloging-in-Publication Data

Knowlton, MaryLee.
    Arriving at Ellis Island / by MaryLee Knowlton and Dale Anderson.
       p. cm. — (Events that shaped America)
    Summary: Describes the experience of immigrants on Ellis Island, where arrivals to the
United States were inspected, processed, and introduced to a life in a new country.
    Includes bibliographical references and index.
    ISBN 0-8368-3221-3 (lib. bdg.)
    1. Ellis Island Immigration Station (N.Y. and N.J.)—History—Juvenile literature.
2. Immigrants—United States—History—Juvenile literature. 3. United States—
Emigration and immigration—History—Juvenile literature. [1. Ellis Island Immigration
Station (N.Y. and N.J.)—History. 2. United States—Emigration and immigration—History.
3. Immigrants—History.] I. Anderson, Dale, 1953- II. Title. III. Series.
JV6484.K57 2002
304.8'73—dc21   2002067026

This North American edition first published in 2002 by
Gareth Stevens Publishing
A World Almanac Education Group Company
330 West Olive Street, Suite 100
Milwaukee, WI 53212 USA

This edition © 2002 by Gareth Stevens Publishing.

Produced by Discovery Books
Editor: Sabrina Crewe
Designer and page production: Sabine Beaupré
Photo researcher: Sabrina Crewe
Maps and diagrams: Stefan Chabluk
Gareth Stevens editorial direction: Mark J. Sachner
Gareth Stevens art direction: Tammy Gruenewald
Gareth Stevens production: Susan Ashley

Photo credits: Corbis: pp. 11, 26, 27; Granger Collection: cover, pp. 4, 18, 23, 25;
Library of Congress: p. 10, 22; North Wind Picture Archives: pp. 5, 9, 12, 13, 14 (top),
New York Public Library: pp. 17, 21; Statue of Liberty National Monument, National
Park Service: pp. 6, 8, 14 (bottom), 15, 16, 19, 20; Ruth Land Sachner, 24.

Printed in the United States of America

1 2 3 4 5 6 7 8 9 06 05 04 03 02

Contents

Introduction

A Nation of Immigrants

In 1892, the U.S. government opened a station on Ellis Island in New York Harbor to process **immigrants**. Many were arriving daily from other countries to make their homes in the United States. At Ellis Island, in view of the Statue of Liberty that welcomed the newcomers, government officials decided who would stay and who would be sent back.

The Start of Immigration

Beginning in the 1500s, people came from Europe, Asia, and Africa to live in the Americas, long before the United States was a nation. Some had come gladly, full of hopes and dreams for a new life. Others had come as captives, torn from their homes in Africa to be sold as slaves in the new land.

This engraving from 1887 shows a group of European immigrants on the deck of a steamship arriving in New York Harbor. There, they caught their first glimpse of the Statue of Liberty.

4

The Golden Door

By the 1840s, the numbers had increased, and between 2 and 3 million were coming in each decade. Between 1820 and 1920, about 33 million immigrants came to the United States. Ellis Island was the doorway to a new home in the United States for many of these immigrants. Because of this, Ellis Island became known as "the Golden Door."

Land of Our Dreams

"My first impression of the new world will always remain etched in my memory, particularly that hazy October morning when I first saw Ellis Island. . . . My mother, my stepfather, my brother . . . and my two sisters . . . all of us together . . . clustered on the foredeck for fear of separation and looked with wonder on this miraculous land of our dreams. . . . Mothers and fathers lifted up the babies so that they too could see, off to the left, the Statue of Liberty. . . . This symbol of America . . . inspired awe in the hopeful immigrants."

Italian immigrant Edward Corsi, describing his arrival in 1907 at the age of ten, In the Shadow of Liberty, *1935*

Chapter One

The Immigrants

These Russian children were brought to the United States in 1908 after their parents were killed in a massacre in their homeland.

No Chance to Get Ahead
"There was absolutely no chance for the common man [in Europe] to get ahead. You just lived, and you finally died, and probably the county had to bury you. We'd have meat about once a year. . . . Once in a while, Mother would buy one of those short bolognas, cut it up, put it in the soup, and everybody would get a little piece. I used to think, 'If [only] I could get enough of that to fill my stomach!'"

Czech immigrant Charles Bartunek, who settled in New York State in 1914

Most **emigrants** to the United States came from Europe where poverty, overcrowding, and **injustice** had made life miserable for millions.

Escaping Persecution and Poverty
Between 1830 and 1840, one-third of new Americans came from Germany. Many were Jews fleeing cruelty in their home country. Later in the century, many more came from eastern Europe and Russia, where soldiers had burned their homes and beaten or killed their families and neighbors.

In Ireland, many people were oppressed by rich English landowners.

The Irish poor survived on potatoes, but the potato crop was struck by disease in 1846. Millions died of starvation, and millions more left the country. From 1841 to 1850, nearly half of the immigrants coming to the United States were Irish.

The Promise of the United States

People fleeing cruelty, poverty, and **persecution** had good reason to hope life would improve in their new land. Earlier immigrants had spread the word. The Europeans knew about the cheap and fertile land they could farm and own for themselves. Canals, factories, and railroads promised jobs for anyone who wanted to work.

A Family's Immigrant Heritage

Vincent Altomare (front left) came to America from southern Italy in 1907 at the age of seventeen, settled in Michigan, and learned to sew. He married Mary Raccosta (front right), who had come from Sicily in 1907 when she was nine years old. They lived in the city of Detroit, where Vincent opened a tailor shop and the couple built a home. Two of their children are pictured here. Their daughter, Gloria, married the son of Swedish immigrants. Their son, Frank, married a woman who came from Scotland.

Chapter Two

Coming to America

Shipping companies issued posters, such as the one on the right, advertising cheap fares. These encouraged people to emigrate to the United States.

Leaving

For many emigrants, the trip to America began months and miles away from a ship. They traveled by train, boat, and horseback, and some even walked, bringing with them as much as they could. From all over the European continent and the British Isles people made their way to the ports. The main European ports were in Liverpool, England; Naples, Italy; and Bremen and Hamburg in Germany.

The Ocean Voyage

When the ship was ready, wealthy travelers boarded first. They slept in cabins and ate in dining rooms. Most of the people, however, traveled in **steerage** class, below the ship's decks surrounded by the ship's steering equipment. As many as two thousand people were crowded into steerage. They slept in large rooms in bunks stacked three high. There was no

German emigrants crowd aboard a ship at the port of Hamburg.

fresh air, not much food, and few toilets or baths. Diseases people brought with them could spread quickly among the travelers. By the time the ship reached New York, many people in steerage were sick, some had died, and everyone was dirty.

In the late 1800s, crossing the Atlantic Ocean became quicker than before, when people had crossed in sailing ships. Using steam power, ships could make the trip in about ten days, whereas sailing ships had taken weeks or months.

The Coffin Ships

Some of the worst conditions were found on what were called the "coffin ships" from Ireland in the 1840s. Over 1.5 million people came to the United States in the 1840s and 1850s to avoid starvation in Ireland. Many, however, were already sick or starving when they boarded their ships. In the close quarters of the ship, disease spread rapidly. Food was in short supply—at that time, passengers had to bring their own food. About one in six Irish people died on the journey across the Atlantic. New laws were passed as a result, and conditions improved a little. From the 1850s, shipowners had to provide food and fresh air.

Journey's End

Finally, the ships drew near New York City. After 1886, as they moved up the Narrows into the Upper Bay, the Statue of Liberty came into sight. This was often an important moment for the immigrants. As one Polish immigrant said:

This photograph, entitled *The Steerage*, shows crowds of passengers on the lower decks of a large passenger ship. The picture was taken by American photographer Alfred Stieglitz when he traveled to Europe in 1907.

"The bigness of Mrs. Liberty overcame us. No one spoke a word, for she was like a goddess and we knew she represented the big, powerful country which was to be our future home."

The Statue of Liberty

In 1886, in celebration of the hundredth anniversary of U.S. independence ten years earlier, France gave the United States a sculpture that symbolized the nation's liberty. After it was installed in New York Harbor, the Statue of Liberty became a symbol of freedom from oppression for generations of immigrants.

The statue, designed by sculptor Frederic Bartholdi, is made of copper sheets over a stainless steel frame and stands 151 feet (46 meters) tall. At its base, these words by the poet Emma Lazarus greet newcomers:

" . . . Give me your tired,
your poor,
Your huddled masses yearning
to breathe free,
The wretched refuse of your
teeming shore.
Send these, the homeless,
tempest-tost to me,
I lift my lamp beside
the golden door!"

Chapter Three

Ellis Island

Immigrants arrive at Castle Garden, the first immigration station in the United States.

Castle Garden

Before 1855, there was no immigration office in New York. People arriving just got off the ship and stayed. Because of the growing number of arrivals, however, New York officials opened a station for processing immigrants in Castle Garden, a building by the harbor. The center soon developed serious problems. There were simply too many people coming in. Also, some officials were **corrupt** and cheated immigrants.

A New Station on Ellis Island

In 1890, the **federal** government took over and began to build an immigration center on a tiny island in New York Harbor. Ellis Island was then only three acres (1.2 hectares) in size.

Ellis Island's Other Names

Native Americans called Ellis Island *Kioshk*, or "Gull Island," after the seabirds that lived there. When Dutch people settled in the area, they harvested shellfish on the island and named it "Little Oyster Island." The island takes its present name from one of its owners, Samuel Ellis. The United States government bought the island in 1808.

Before constructing buildings, the engineers had to work on the island itself to make it bigger. They doubled its size, using the earth removed from tunnels that were being dug for New York City's subway system. By making a channel in the harbor floor, they also deepened the water around the island so large ships could dock there. Docks that could host two large ships at a time were built in front of the main building.

The First Buildings

The main processing center was a wooden building designed to handle ten thousand people and twelve thousand pieces of luggage a day. The government also built a hospital, a laundry, and a power plant. Old buildings that had been used earlier by the U. S. Army were turned into dormitories.

On January 1, 1892, a young Irish girl named Annie Moore became the first immigrant to land on Ellis Island. She was greeted by the new commissioner of immigration, who gave her a ten-dollar gold piece, the most money she had ever seen.

This early photograph of the Ellis Island immigration center shows the original wooden buildings that opened in 1892.

Poor immigrant families, such as this one at Ellis Island in 1901, became targets for Americans who resented foreigners coming to live in the United States.

New Immigration Laws

Now that the federal government was in charge of immigration, it began to limit who could come. Despite the poem on the Statue of Liberty calling for the poor and tired from other lands, Congress passed laws barring **paupers**, criminals, people with mental illnesses or infectious diseases, and people likely to need government help. In 1906, Congress created the Bureau of Immigration to take charge of Ellis Island.

This view of Ellis Island today shows the buildings constructed after the fire of 1897. At the top left are islands added in 1899 and 1906. They have been joined together.

Fire

Only five years after the station opened, a fire destroyed all the buildings on Ellis Island. Although no one died, all the immigration records from 1855 to 1890 burned. In 1900, the complex reopened and a whole new island had been added. This time, the buildings had been made of brick and iron.

Ellis Island's Workers

A complex that handled ten thousand people each day needed workers to do many types of jobs. Ellis Island had dockers on the docks and maintenance workers in the buildings. There were cooks, maids, nurses, doctors, telegraph operators, and interpreters, as well as immigration inspectors. In busy years, each inspector processed five hundred people a day.

Besides the paid workers, there were volunteers on the island. Many were there to greet and help people from their home countries. Others were members of religious groups who came to welcome people of the same religion.

Ellis Island workers in the early 1920s.

Chapter Four

Through the Golden Door

INSPECTION CARD

(Immigrants and Steerage Passengers).

Port of departure, DANZIG. S. S. Estonia

Name of ship,

Name of Immigrant,

Date of departure,

Last residence,

The East-Asiatic Company, Limited.

BALTIC AMERICA LINE.

Inspected and passed ad

DANZIG.

UNITED STATES

PUBLIC HEALTH SERVICE

Medical Officer

(The following to be filled in by ship's surgeon or agent prior to or after embarcation).

Ship's list or manifest

Berth No.

Passed at quarantine, port of

Passed by Immigration Bureau

port of

SENT TO HOSPITAL

DEC 1925

No. on ship's list or manifest

No. 37c. 5000. 5. 24.

This inspection card was issued to a Polish immigrant in 1925.

Arriving

When immigrants arrived in New York, they did not all have to go through Ellis Island. Inspectors boarded incoming ships to make quick checks of the passengers in first and second class and allowed them to enter the United States. The poorer people, those who had traveled in steerage, proceeded to Ellis Island for a more critical examination.

As they left the ferries that brought them from the ship to the island, the new immigrants carried all their belongings.

A New Name

Many people say that Ellis Island inspectors who could not understand their foreign, unfamiliar names changed them to something simpler. Historians doubt this, knowing that inspectors compared names to ships' records, where the immigrants' full, correct names were recorded, and could just copy them. Also, many inspectors also spoke another language or worked with interpreters. It is true that many immigrants took new names in the United States. Why did that happen? Some historians say that the immigrants probably changed their names soon after they arrived to something sounding more American.

These were left in the baggage room of the main building. Many were afraid to leave their trunks and bags, which contained everything they owned in the world.

The immigrants all had a card pinned to their clothes. Each card had the person's name, the name of his or her ship, and the page number where the person was listed in the ship's records.

The Medical Inspection

The first step for the new immigrants was the medical inspection. They had all heard about this, and everyone feared failing the exam or being separated from family members who failed. From the moment the immigrants entered the room, they were watched by the inspectors for signs of physical disability or illness. Not all conditions were reason for being refused entry. Some people were treated in the Ellis Island hospitals until they were well enough to enter the country.

Inspectors looked carefully for an eye disease called trachoma, which could lead to blindness and spread easily from one person to another. Doctors lifted the eyelids of each person, in a quick but sometimes painful movement. Anyone with trachoma was refused entry.

An Italian family stands in the luggage hall, surrounded by their belongings. The new arrivals are about to start the Ellis Island process.

Immigrants are lining up for an eye inspection. The medical inspector lifts up an immigrant's eyelid to check for trachoma.

By 1917, a person could be refused entry for fifty different medical reasons. Doctors chalked a letter on the back of rejected candidates that indicated what problems they saw. The letter "L" meant lame, "H" meant heart problems, and "B" meant a bad back. But after a second exam, many of these people were allowed to enter.

The Interview

The second step was the interview. The inspectors asked each immigrant many questions. The first few questions were easy: name, place of birth, job, and whether they were joining relatives already here. No answer to these simple questions would be a reason to turn down the immigrant.

The next questions were trickier. Each person was asked who had paid his or her passage. People who had not paid for their own passage were excluded unless they were joining family, because they were considered too poor. Inspectors also asked immigrants if they held certain kinds of opinions. People with strong political views were excluded because they might cause trouble.

Refused Entry

Being turned away at Ellis Island meant the end of a dream for the immigrant. A parent had to go back with any child under twelve years old. Parents had to decide on the spot how they would split up their families. As terrible as it was, not many people—only about 1 percent—were refused entry.

People at Ellis Island waited in long lines in the large registry room for their turn to be interviewed by an immigration official.

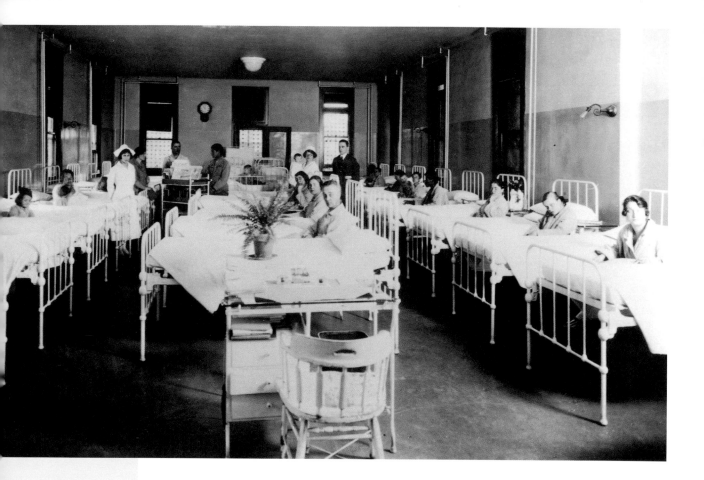

People arriving seriously ill at Ellis Island were treated in the island's hospitals. This is a women's ward in one of the hospitals.

Detainees

Many more people faced being **detained**. If they arrived sick, they were held in the hospitals. Some were held until relatives arrived to meet them or sent them money for boat or train fares to their new homes. An unmarried woman had to wait to be claimed by a male relative or a man who was going to marry her. Many weddings took place on Ellis Island for this reason. Some detainees had to wait for relatives or friends to arrive and vouch for their good character.

Detainees slept on cots or bunks in cramped dormitories. When there were too many of them at one time, some detainees slept on floors and benches. The detainees were given food, but it was not always good. Often it was not the same kind of food they had eaten in their homelands.

Being detained after such a long trip with the end so near at hand was disappointing for the immigrants. But it was better than being sent back. For many, it was also better than what they had left behind.

Admitted

There are many stories of people who were sent back or detained, but most people passed through Ellis Island in just a few hours. They were given papers stamped "admitted" and they were released. Some happily joined their waiting friends and family. Others traveled alone by train into New York City or nearby New Jersey to begin new lives.

International Menu
"If I [served] spaghetti, the detained Italians sent me [thanks] and everybody else objected. If I put **pierogi** and **mazovian noodles** on the table, the Poles were happy and the rest [unhappy]. Irish stew was no good for the English and . . . English **marmalade** was gunpowder to the Irish."

Henry Curran, commissioner of Ellis Island from 1923 to 1926

People were sometimes detained on Ellis Island for long periods, even for months. By 1914, there were play-grounds and recreation areas and even teachers for child detainees.

Chapter Five

Life in a New Land

Starting a New Life

With the inspection at Ellis Island behind them, newly arrived immigrants faced the truly hard work of building the rest of their lives. Many also faced prejudice from Americans who had been in the United States for generations. People descended from earlier immigrant groups—those who came from Germany and Britain, for instance—felt they were better than the new immigrants from eastern and southern Europe.

There was plenty of work. Immigrant workers made iron, steel, and locomotives, and they built skyscrapers and bridges. They made clothing and shoes, packed meat, and canned

This is New York City's Mulberry Street in 1900. The street, with its bustling market, was a center for European immigrants, particularly those from Italy and eastern Europe.

Members of an immigrant family live and work in a tenement building. The whole family, even the children, worked at making cigars.

vegetables. The work was hard, dangerous, and often low paying. But the immigrants' hard work often paid off, and over time many of them improved their lot.

Poverty in the Cities

Most immigrants moved to parts of U.S. cities that had been settled by others from their home country. **Tenement** buildings sprang up to house all these new people, and the cities soon became crowded and unhealthy. In the late 1800s and early 1900s, **social reformers** fought for services to improve the living and working conditions of the newest Americans.

Streets Paved with Gold
"I came to America because I heard the streets were paved with gold. When I got here, I found out three things. First, the streets were not paved with gold. Second, they weren't paved at all. Third, I was expected to pave them."

A joke told by Italian Americans

Hyman Landsman and Rose Kaplan were young Jews who both came through Ellis Island around 1910. They are shown here with their daughters Ruth, Florence, and Marian. Although they had lived near each other in Lithuania, Hy and Rose had not known each other until they met in the States. Hyman changed his name from Landsman to Land and married Rose. The Lands settled down in Bristol, Connecticut, where Hy, a tailor, started his own men's clothing store.

The Lands' daughters grew up as Americans, and their Jewish identity took a back seat to their desire to blend in with non-Jewish friends. The three girls married and had children of their own who are proud to be American Jews. By the time Hy and Rose died in the 1970s, their grandchildren had begun asking about their lives in Europe.

Moving West

Other immigrants left the cities behind them for regions that were less populated. They headed for the Midwest and the Great Plains, where they could pay a small fee to claim 160 acres (69 ha) of land. After farming the land for five years, they owned it outright. This was called homesteading, and thousands of immigrant families became homesteaders.

On the Plains

The promise of nearly free land was bright, but the work was hard. Everyone in the family worked to produce crops on land prone to drought, flood, fire, and plagues of insects. The farms were often far from each other, and life could be very lonely.

Still, these new settlers were soon supplying the whole country with corn, wheat, vegetables, and dairy products.

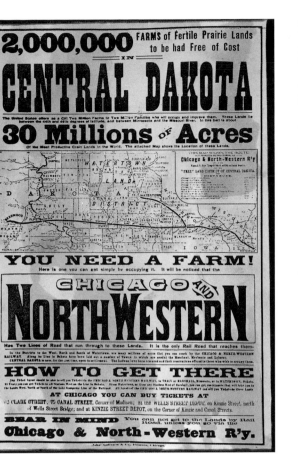

This is the kind of poster that greeted immigrants on their arrival in the United States. The promise of farmland encouraged many to leave the cities and head west.

Ethnic Communities

The settlers also formed their own communities, much as the immigrants did in city neighborhoods. In larger cities, there were Italian, Jewish, Polish, Irish, and Asian communities. In the midwestern states, towns grew up that had the influences of immigrants from Norway, Germany, Sweden, and Denmark.

Building America

"Most of the immigrants came to these shores without a penny. But they are the ones who have built the palaces, machines, food, and clothing which America enjoys today."

From the Jewish Daily Forward, *a New York-based Yiddish-language newspaper, 1909*

Excess Quota

"[At the docks] were 2,000 men, women and children who were 'excess quota.' Here, by our country's permission, the 2,000 would now be turned back. . . . I could only watch them go. Day by day, the barges took them from Ellis Island back to the ships again, back to the ocean, back to what? As they trooped aboard the big barges under my window, carrying their heavy bundles, . . . they twisted something in my heart that hurts to this day."

Henry Curran, commissioner of Ellis Island from 1923 to 1926

The Golden Door Closes

In the early 1920s, the U.S. government began to use **quotas** to decide how many immigrants could come from each country. Because of the quotas, the number of immigrants dropped to fewer than thirty thousand a year by the 1930s.

By the 1940s, Ellis Island was no longer needed to process new Americans because so few people were arriving. In 1954, Ellis Island was closed.

During World War II, U.S. citizens such as these German Americans were taken to Ellis Island as detainees because they had been born in countries that were at war with the United States.

Reopening Ellis Island

The years were hard on the buildings on Ellis Island. The harsh New York winters and lack of upkeep left broken windows, moldy walls, and rotten wood floors. In the 1980s, however, Ellis Island was restored, and it reopened as an immigration museum in 1990. Today, more than two million people every year pass through Ellis Island, but now they come as tourists.

The Ellis Island museum is housed in what was once the main immigration building. It has been restored inside and out.

Immigration Today

In 1965, the United States government began lifting the restrictions that had been placed on immigration in the 1920s. Since then, nearly 25 million people have come to the United States. Today, most of the immigrants are Asian or Hispanic. The countries from which most immigrants come are Mexico, the Philippines, Russia, and China.

The Wall of Honor

Outside the Ellis Island museum stands the Wall of Honor. Cut into the wall are the names of more than 600,000 immigrants to the United States. Any person, for a fee, can have the names of his or her ancestors added to this landmark, even if they did not come through Ellis Island. The Wall of Honor honors all immigrants who came to the United States and helped build a nation. It is the biggest wall of names in the world.

Time Line

1808	U.S. government obtains Ellis Island.
1840s	Immigrants start coming to the United States in large numbers.
1855	New York State opens an immigration station at Castle Garden.
1880s	Immigration reaches new highs.
1886	France gives the Statue of Liberty to the United States.
1890	Federal government takes over control of immigration in New York. Construction work begins at Ellis Island.
1891	Congress passes laws that bar certain people from entering the United States.
1892	Immigration center opens on Ellis Island.
1897	Buildings on Ellis Island are destroyed by fire.
1900	Rebuilt immigration station opens on Ellis Island.
1906	Bureau of Immigration is established.
1907	Busiest year at Ellis Island, with more than 1 million immigrants processed. April 17: Busiest single day at Ellis Island, with 11,747 immigrants processed.
1921	Congress passes new law to limit immigration with quotas.
1924	Congress further limits immigration.
1940s	Ellis Island is used to hold "enemy aliens."
1954	Ellis Island is closed.
1983	Restoration of Ellis Island buildings begins.
1990	Ellis Island Immigration Museum opens.
1998	U.S. Supreme Court rules that most of Ellis Island (consisting of land that was created by landfill) actually falls within the borders of New Jersey, not New York.

Things to Think About and Do

Immigrant Families

Ask a parent or other relative about your ancestors. Did anyone in your family come to America as an immigrant? When did they come? Where did they come from? How did they arrive? Did they pass through Ellis Island? Where did they settle and what did they do in their new homes? Find out the names of your immigrant ancestors if you can, and write their story.

Scrapbook

Visit the American Family History Immigration Center (www.ellisisland.org) online. Read through one or more of the "family scrapbooks" on the web site. Make a list of things that you would want to include in a scrapbook of your family's history.

At Ellis Island

Read Chapter Four about going through the Ellis Island process. Imagine that you are an immigrant who has just arrived with your mother, and your father is waiting for you. Make a list of the various stages of the Ellis Island process and write a diary entry for each one. Are you frightened? What does it feel like to be in a foreign country for the first time? How do the immigration inspectors and other workers treat you?

Glossary

corrupt: not honest when doing an official job. Some officials at Castle Garden and Ellis Island were corrupt because they cheated immigrants in money exchanges and overcharged them for rail tickets and services.

detain: keep back.

emigrant: person leaving home to go and live somewhere else.

federal: to do with the national government of the United States.

immigrant: person coming to a new country or region to live.

injustice: something that is unfair.

marmalade: sweet orange jelly very popular with British people.

mazovian noodles: pasta made of a special kind of flour.

pauper: person with no money or possessions and no means of support except for charity.

persecution: the causing of suffering to people, usually because they are different from the people who are persecuting them.

pierogi: fried Polish dumplings filled with meat, cheese, or vegetables.

quota: set amount. In the case of immigration, foreign countries had a quota of people who would be allowed to enter the United States every year.

social reformer: person who tries to make changes in society that help people.

steerage: section of a ship below decks where the steering equipment is and where people traveled if they did not have enough money for a cabin.

tempest-tost: tossed about in a storm.

tenement: crowded and badly built apartment house, often unsafe and unhealthy to live in.

tuberculosis: fatal disease that affects the lungs.

Further Information

Books

Freedman, Russell. *Immigrant Kids*. Scott Foresman, 1995.

Levine, Ellen. *If Your Name Was Changed at Ellis Island*. Scholastic, 1994.

Nixon, Joan Lowery. *Land of Dreams (Ellis Island Stories)*. Gareth Stevens, 2001.

Nixon, Joan Lowery. *Land of Hope (Ellis Island Stories)*. Gareth Stevens, 2001.

Nixon, Joan Lowery. *Land of Promise (Ellis Island Stories)*. Gareth Stevens, 2001.

Wolfman, Ira. *Do People Grow on Family Trees? Genealogy for Kids and Other Beginners*. Workman Publishing, 1991.

Web Sites

www.ellisisland.com Information about and pictures of exhibits at the immigration museum on Ellis Island.

www.nps.gov/elis/ National Park Service offers information about Ellis Island National Monument.

www.ellisisland.org American Family History Immigration Center offers archive of Ellis Island's records in which users can find information about ancestors who came through the island between 1892 and 1924.

Useful Addresses

Statue of Liberty Ellis Island National Monument
National Park Service
Liberty Island
New York, NY 10004
Telephone: (212) 363-3206

Index

Page numbers in **bold** indicate pictures.